Dwell

Dwell is the second print book published by South Broadway Press. Proceeds raised from the sale of this book will go to support **The Village Institute, a live/learn/work center for refugees and immigrants in Aurora, Colorado, USA.**

Learn more about The Village Institute at www.sites.google.com/view/villageinstitute/home.

We respectfully acknowledge that this book was created on the traditional, ancestral, unceded territory of the Cheyenne, Arapaho, and Ute People who have stewarded this land through generations.

An Anthology of Poetry Supporting The Village Institute

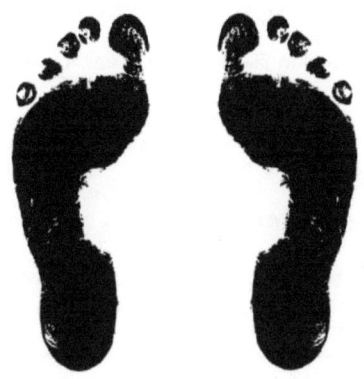

South Broadway Press | Denver CO

SOUTH BROADWAY PRESS

Published by South Broadway Press
South Broadway Press LLC, 1350 Josephine St Denver CO 80206, USA

First published in the United States of America by South Broadway Press, 2022

Copyright © South Broadway Press, 2022
All rights reserved

Poems in this anthology have appeared previously in the following places:

"Home"; Ferganchick,Caleb; Slamming Bricks Anthology

Cover Image: Mohaddeseh Seyyed Nouri

THE LIBRARY OF CONGRESS HAS CATALOGED THE PAPERBACK
EDITION AS FOLLOWS:
Press, South Broadway
Dwell: An Anthology of Poetry Supporting The Village Institute

ISBN (pbk.) 978-1-7350355-9-8

Printed in the United States of America

Edited by
Emylee Frank, Kali Love Heals, Terra Iverson,
Huascar Medina, Brice Maiurro, Sarah Rodriguez

Except in the United States of America, this book is sold subject to the condition that it shall not, by way of trade or otherwise, be lent, re-sold, hired out, or otherwise circulated without the publisher's prior consent in any form of binding or cover other than that which it is published and without a similar condition including this condition being imposed on the subsequent purchaser.

The scanning, uploading and distribution of this book via the Internet or via any other means without the permission of the publisher is illegal and punishable by law. Please purchase online authorized electronic editions, and do not participate in or encourage electronic piracy of copyrighted materials. Your support of the authors' rights is appreciated.

www.soboghoso.org

www.sites.google.com/view/villageinstitute/home

Dwell

An Anthology of Poems Supporting The Village Institute

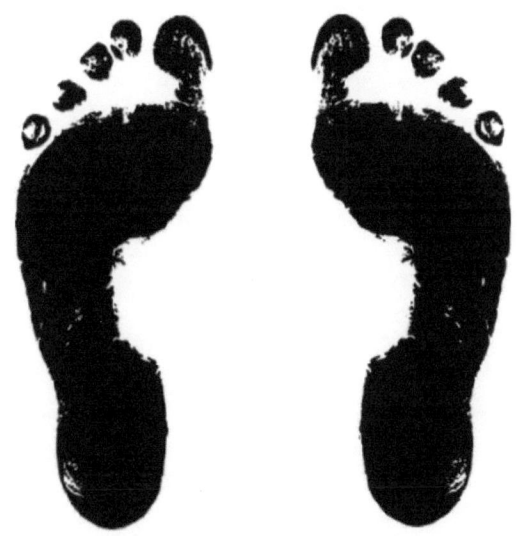

Edited By:
Emylee Frank, Kali Love Heals, Terra Iverson,
Brice Maiurro, Huascar Medina & Sarah Rodriguez

ON BEING A HOME
A Poem by Ellie Adelman, Founder & Executive Director of The Village Institute

My people were… are…
wanderers
through deserts
to mountain tops
from villages
to ghettos
to ships across miles of blue-black
treacherous ocean
Everything wrapped in woven fabric
Later bound tightly to bodies, cloaked beneath layers
to keep warm, to keep hidden
One day packed carefully in cardboard boxes
loaded onto a truck
the size of our ancestors' entire homes

That search for home…
transporting
that little collection of treasures
of memories
of tradition and heirlooms
brought from the motherland
or at least those who have touched its soil
It is all too familiar
I know what it is to search
to always be searching
for home

But how can I
a child of wanderers

know what it is
to *be* a home?

I am learning
We are
slowly

Just like those small treasures
secreted away
It is the little things
It is setting the table
with food that tastes like
we never remember not knowing the taste
It is dancing to the rhythm
to the words
our bodies recognize
like our own heartbeat
our own breath
It is making space
on a wall, a shelf
for those little treasures
for photos, for drawings, for colors and script
that reflect back to us
where
and who
we will always be from

It is also the big things
the deep things
It is patience with ourselves
with each other
as we learn to relearn
everything

and hold onto
something
anything
however we can
It is pretending
to be just a little calmer than we feel
for those not so far
along the path
from leaving home
to finding it,
lending a sister
our nervous system
for a moment
in case she forgot
in case she lost
that feeling of what it is
to be safe
It is helping a mother find
build
what she needs
to help her children
settle in
settle down
but never
settle
It is finding a way forward
and a way back
all at once

We are all born
with flesh and blood
that remember
a village

somewhere
For some of us
the memory is buried deep
deep within the story
of whom we *think* we are
For others it is still visible
through the dust
in the rear-view mirror

For now
for us
this is ours
Our village
of many mothers
of children
living between two worlds
of pain and joy
and dreams
of what we may become
together
separately
This village may not yet
feel like home
be home
to each of us
to all of us
But we are here
learning
that all it really is
is to *be for*
each other.

A Note From Kali Love Heals
South Broadway Press Editor

This collection is filled with thoughts to get lost in. Ideas to call home. Laughter. Vulnerability that makes you think. So much truth. And, also like my life, faeries!

I've been dwelling on the idea of home a lot these days, and I keep thinking of those without. Refugees and immigrants come to America for asylum, hoping for a better life. And many find it, but it's a hard-won possibility. The world is facing so much turmoil and unrest right now that there is more migration in the last year than we have seen in decades. So what do we do? We live another year on Earth, dwelling dangerously, acting as lovingly as we can. With a handful of people—non-astronaut people—even doing so together in space for the first time.

The semi-post-Covid world is perhaps a bit lighter as we get to be physically close to one another again. Hugs are back, people! And though there are still a few elbows and masks that just may stick around, we are thrilled to be grounded by touch and moved by words in community again.

I would like to thank our brave poets for their beautiful offerings and to thank you, dear reader, for taking the time to read and support these writers, The Village Institute, and us here at South Broadway Press and Ghost Society. Herein find hope when walking through hell and heart to give you as much grace as you can allow yourself to have. Please enjoy this collection. You deserve it!

A Note From LiveWork Denver
Financial sponsor of *Dwell*

When our LiveWork Denver team learned South Broadway Press planned to publish a poetry anthology on the theme of housing, we were intrigued. When we found out the proceeds would go to The Village Institute, we knew we wanted to get involved.

We are profoundly grateful to the team at South Broadway Press for all of their work to bring this anthology to life and to The Village Institute for their ongoing commitment to creating a living, working, and creative place for refugee and immigrant families. Supporting creatives and efforts to increase housing in our community are at the core of what we do.

We know how important secure and stable housing is for the wellbeing of our community. As housing prices increase and wages don't keep up, it's often artists, creatives, entrepreneurs, nonprofit professionals, immigrants, and refugees who are pushed out of Denver and move to surrounding cities in search of more affordable places to live. But it's exactly these community members who bring such richness, creativity, and hope for the future of our city.

We know there is a deep need for innovation in housing. We also know there is great opportunity at the intersection of housing and community. That's why we are committed to helping people explore creative pathways towards home ownership, while also fostering community, through opportunities like cooperatives, cohousing, cobuying, and live/work spaces.

Through innovative approaches to buying, selling, and investing in real estate, our LiveWork Denver team matches people with living spaces that help them become the fullest expression of themselves. Supporting the Dwell Anthology and The Village Institute is what our motto, "real estate for the greater good" is all about. To learn more about LiveWork Denver, please visit our website www.liveworkdenever.com.

In gratitude,
Laura, Sarah, and Bri
LiveWork Denver: Real Estate for the Greater Good

Table Of Contents

APARTMENT	3
Wheeler Light	
ROOMS	4
Liza Sparks	
HOMESICK	6
M. Palowski Moore	
STRANGE, WHAT FABRIC THE BODY CAN BE	8
Jade Lascelles	
TRANSPLANTING	12
Lillian Fuglei	
YOU ARE NOT THE FATHER	14
Jozer Guerrero	
WALKING	16
Jozer Guerrero	
PANSEY TO PALE	21
Liam Max Kelley	
SOLITUDE	22
Dee Allen	
NO TRESPASS	23
Rue Kream	
YOUR CURRENT GPS LOCATION	24
Jason Ryberg	
LET US PRAY	25
reb	
POTS & PANS	26
Zack Kopp	
A CONDITION WITHOUT GHOSTS	28
Abigail Chabitnoy	
THE MOTHER OF THE OXFORD ENGLISH DICTIONARY	30
Allison Maschoff	
HOUSE OF MY HEART	31
Taylor Jones	
TELL IT SLANT	32
Cortney Collins	
HOUSE OF BLUES	34
Susan Carman	

CARVED INTO HOME	35
Hayden Dansky	
MOONLIT SLABS OF LIGHT...	37
Crisosto Apache	
A POEM WHICH MAY BE MISTAKEN...	39
Said Shaiye	
A SPECIAL PLACE	42
Norbert Góra	
FLOOR BARE	43
Jessica Rigney	
LEAN HOME	45
Jessica Rigney	
PROGRESS, MEXICO	46
Dustin King	
THE OLD HOMESTEAD	50
M. Palowski Moore	
DELAYED HOMECOMING	53
Jayati Das	
SUBURBAN MANDALA	55
Boyd Bauman	
THE HOUSE WE BUILD TOGETHER	57
Christopher Clauss	
I AM TRYING TO REMEMBER IF I MARRIED FOR LOVE	59
Kimberly Ann Priest	
AUGUST A PLACE	61
Lori Brack	
MOVING THROUGH	62
Wheeler Light	
THE IDUKKI DAM	65
Anu Lal	
DAYS OF RED AND GOLD	67
David Estringel	
WHERE WILL WE DWELL?	69
Destiny Armstrong	
PORTRAIT OF A BEDROOM WALL	70
Andrew Walker	
HOME	71
Caleb Ferganchick	
HOUSE SONG	74
Aerik Francis	

Dwell

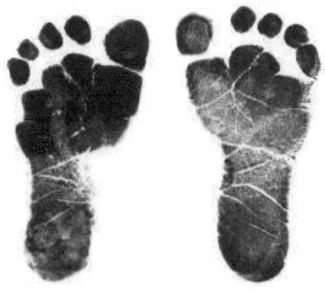

Apartment
Wheeler Light

You open the apartment door and it is just wood. Wood behind the door. You need to enter your apartment. To sleep. To work. To clean. You burrow into the wood with a small drill bore. You carve a desk inside the wood. You leave legs of the wood in each corner of the room so the wood roof doesn't collapse on you, crushed by mahogany in the night. You wake one day and it is raining paper. A hole has split in the wood from all the paper where it was leaking from the bathtub upstairs. The paper is covered in all your upstairs neighbor's poetry. Your upstairs neighbor is always so loud, crying for whole weeks at a time. Your neighbor is so loud the sound bleeds through the mahogany. The mahogany is now spilling into your bed, your bed you carved yourself out of the desk, the desk which appeared behind the door, the apartment which was drowned in poetry. The future that is always words.

Rooms
Liza Sparks

"I dwell in Possibility—"
  -Emily Dickinson

               Every
          body has a right
        to shelter in a home.
    To be safe from cold, the heat,
             the storm.

///

We want a house built by the people / we want walls of justice /
we want liberation / we want windows and doors of possibility /
look outside / in a world where everyone has a home /
anything is possible / how do we transform /

///

"Home is where the heart is." The heart is the size of your fist.
Some things are worth fighting for.

///

Homelessness is not a choice.
Criminalizing survival is unconstitutional.[1]

///

The body—
my body is made of rooms of memory—
The body—
my body is made of hallways—
The body—

my body does not remember—
The body—
my body remembers everything

                ///

Here is my skin. Imagine all of the things I have touched.
Here are my bones.

                ///

I do not remember leaving the dwelling of my mother's body.
I do not remember being born.

                ///

What does it mean to care for another?

[1]denverhomelessoutloud.org

Homesick
M. Palowski Moore

I am dreaming of
An Alabama night—
Crickets chirping; echoing
Of sentiment, breaking
The song of the loon
Diving, strutting
Through phrases, phases
Of a honeysuckle
Milk glass moon
Whose distant sway
Ripples, pools, pulls
Pebbled ponds, precious pearls
Where locals gather
To swim, fish, skip stones
Across reflections of sky and stars.

I am. falling, failing—
Form fleeing a cold city
An asp escaping
This fruitless orchard
A moth chained by the
Candlelight of a distant beacon.

I close my eyes
See the pines, skies
White wings, fluttering
Glittering patchwork
Transforming. I am again
A small-town boy

Taking the back road,
Wooded path winding
To the Jackson-Slaughter bridge;
Racing in the pecan grove,
Chasing shadows, fireflies;
Laughing, dreaming, laying
Staring, believing—feeling
The force; the iron vein
Of a vanishing home—
Remembering more from
Windows that never close
A place I no longer belong.

STRANGE, WHAT FABRIC THE BODY CAN BE
Jade Lascelles

the materiality, texture layered atop itself

    bristling old wool shorn and barbed from so much wear. knitted with cheap

    yarn, the acrylic kind that tightens too much, squeaks after

    time and so many washes. a thick polyester clinging to the body

    odor of the great aunt who first wore it. a light chiffon scarf

    draped, artful but nonchalant. a coat patched too obviously.

    stinking of the mothballs from a long-untouched winter closet.

how you are sewn into it

    how you drive around a town you have not lived in for fifteen years. the

streets so foreign for the first few days. you, without clear
compass or

signpost. home, a place of now-unfamiliar intersections.
until on the

third day you feel a strange tug. a too-tight stitch pulling
beneath the

muscles in your chest. a breath caught in the button of
your throat.

because you suddenly know these storefronts, just with
different

names. because you remember the shape and weight of
who still

patterns the pavement below. who forever married a part
of you to

this neighborhood. whose cord has been knotted to yours
all along. you

have driven frightfully close to where something terrible
happened. until

now you forgot the event even took place in a house at all.
it existing

all this time only in the unnamable space of your hazy
recollections.

and the stains it collects, the memory

every time you put on the shirt, your eyes go right to the
small spot of

redness. you know the exact meal you were eating. how
you were sitting at

a not proper dining space. how the sauce splashed when
the pot boiled

over. how her homemade jam was thinner and dripped
more. when the

brown corduroy got that conspicuous patch of dried glue
along the front

most thigh. the leaking pen. the accident. the accidental.
that which

you pick at and sniff at and rub in and soak with hopes of
it fading more.

how you wear it, but also, how you are woven of it

you sense the distinct tastes inside your mouth whenever
you look at the

photo. it is almost unbelievable now, teaching
kindergartners to cook.

trusting such small and wild hands with knives to chop
the radishes, a hot

griddle to fry up tortillas. you made butter as a class,
taking turns shaking

the mason jar of cream. the excited aggression you all
stifled around pet gerbils

and younger siblings having found an escape. a riot of
children given task

and purpose for their agitation. you hold a photo of this
day, see your own

smile as you chew a bit of buttered bread. see how you
once delighted

so in it. how delicious it could be, the violence of so many
hands.

Transplanting
Lillian Fuglei

Prune the leaves—pluck
the crisp ones that no longer
serve her, watch them
hit the floor with a bone crunch.
Gently untangle
her vines from their previous
cage. Dislocate her
from one pot,
descending to the next.

We place her
into the soil. Pearlite
and peat moss, spilling past
the edges of her new shelter, dusting
your Pine-Sol purified floor.

Pat her down, our hands meet
under the dirt, a brush
of unearned domesticity.
Specks of soil, line
the ridges of your fingertips,
granting anonymity
to your palms.

Sitting
knee to knee, surrounding
her dwelling. I gaze
into your eyes
and wonder, will this be her final

resting place? Or will we uproot,
disrupt her growth, push her
past the point of no return?

You Are Not The Father
Jozer Guerrero

The results are in in the case of America Christopher Columbus you are not the father I am writing this poem on Columbus Day picking at scabs from Old Wounds that have yet to heal reading old history textbooks for inspiration if there's anything more painful than an old white guy telling your story it's when it's wrongfully told I still remember the first time I learned his name my teacher's words sounded more like a rifle Christopher Columbus discovered America that moment I felt the Thunder beings crack the sky I was in first grade and even then I understood that something was missing so I raised my hand and somehow it felt like an Indian revolt like I was shooting wooden arrows into the mouth of a steel Canon what about the Indians how can you discover someone when Mother Earth already spoke their name into existence and mr. Washington's eyes turned into smallpox and the blankets ready to exterminate any question that I had well the Indians were just a bunch of heathens undressed and uncivilized and suddenly our classroom turned into the battle at the Little Bighorn and the ancestors said today is a good day to die and I'll be damned if I let these motherfuckers lie but I was 7 years old excluded from Thanksgiving dinner scoldings I received felt like a massacre at Sand Creek like braids being cut off at boarding school they say the only good Indian is a dead Indian Ghost can I pray in their own language so they cut our hands off if we didn't bring enough gold and if you really wish to exterminate the Savages you must start with their children because nits make lice and lice are bloodthirsty but here's the irony when Columbus first encountered the tainos he gave us the name Ingles meaning in God for God's children someone please explain to me why we worship a man who kills angels I guess he read the Bible the same way you read map coordinates with his eyes closed yet today we still celebrate the world's biggest mistake the truth is Columbus never even stepped foot on what we call America yes bloody Spirit still lives on in the hungry trigger fingers of police officers killing Indians at a higher rate than any other racial group in America through oil pipelines that stretch themselves to our reservations polluting our water supply America is there not enough blood underneath your fingernails are ready you have tried so hard to bury it underground but you forgot that we were seeds are red tree was still Blossom and you will never cut us down

WALKING
Jozer Guerrero

I got that special type of walk

The type of walk your

Daddy used when he first talked to your

Mama type of walk

Yea!

I got that special type of lean

So smooth you'd think I'm cruising a low-rider

On Cinco de Mayo

See, I've been waiting on my walk for a while now

Ever since I was a little chavalito

I can recall my father walking me through the process

At an early age, he would say

Walking is one of the simplest ways you could show someone

Your freedom

"See, the first step to being enslaved is to actually get caught!

Why do you think Martin Luther King Jr and Cesar Chavez

Spent all that time marching!?"

"You have to stay on your toes, Mijo

This system has interesting ways of turning a man into a slave"

If you asked my father for a ride

He would tell you to

Walk

After crossing the desert for a better life

My father sees my walk to any Open Mic

As an easy stroll through the park walking

In my father's footsteps has taught me that

If you love something you will do anything you

Can to get to it

Your feet will get you there if you allow them to

My father walks with the determination of an immigrant

Like his children will starve if he doesn't walk fast enough

Like there are immigration agents chasing after him

He is America's worst nightmare

A bad ass in a foreign country and I

Always wanted to walk just like him but

I always seem to take the wrong steps

Walking in and out of Jail

Pacing in my cell like a caged Ocelot

These must have been the ways you get

Enslaved my father talked about and

It all started in the seventh grade when doctors

Explained to my parents why I walked with a slight limp

My right leg was shorter than the left

Forcing me to apply most of my body weight on the right side

I developed a walk that would quickly label me a thug

I guess the inequalities I was exposed to finally

Drenched through my clothes and into my bones

So now I walk like I got a wounded knee

Like the structure holds me down by my back pockets

Saggy jeans are one of the side effects left over

From my oppression and

When you walk with this much weight at an

Early age your steps

Begin to sound like ticking bombs

The type of walk that'd make a motherfucker

Move out the way the type of walk

That'd make a cop want to follow you

In 2012 Trayvon Martin

and all the years after

Mike Brown

Eric Gardner

Jessie Hernandez

Sandra Bland

George Floyd was murdered for

Having the same walk as me

Trayvon was only 17

They asked me why I cried

Because he walked just like me

Because he was just like me!

Still perfecting his own walk still getting use to the

Feeling of walking in a black man's shoes

This is the reason why boys like us

Never achieved social mobility

How can we climb the ladders of class if we can't even

Walk through our neighborhoods without feeling like

Someone is chasing after us

But I'll risk it all to show my son and the rest of the

Chavalitos in the world that we can walk to a

Better future instead of having to walk away from everything

That we can walk across the stage and graduate

Instead of having to walking in front of a judge

That if we all walk at the same time

The weight of our steps would force the world to flip its rotation

So stand up and walk with me

We have the world at our feet I think it's time

That we exercise our freedom

Pansey to Pale
Liam Max Kelley

My books in our apartment
                      have faded a different color
Dark spines now shades of lavender
the titles have gone
               from pansy to pale
Even when she fingers the blinds
closed all day
          light finds a way
to wear ink thin
             To combat excess
new vines dangle ubiquitous
Over each shelf
         a graveyard
with shadows tucked
             kitty-corner portraits
Sometimes I rotate the words
less direct sunlight
             spells a shared wear-and-tear
My toenails shine orange
       after I've painted them
           with antifungal polish
and her paintings each are purple
after she combined
         cracked makeup
with acrylic medium
When we moved in
             we called it eclectic
Now I forget what my books look like
until she opens a window

SOLITUDE
Dee Allen

Lack of a lover
Lack of children
Lack of pets
Lack of flatmates
Lack of arguments
Starting out petty
Lack of partitioned space
Lack of visitors
Unless they're invited—
Just me
In my little house
Two room
Inner sanctum
Where I could be
Just me—
A living
Situation
I seem
Condemned to
& somehow

Prefer—

No Trespass
Rue Kream

They built a cabin, near the woods
At the back of their land, of lumber
Cut and shaped with bare hands.
A candle, a table, a bed beneath a
Canopy of constellations.

It stood beside the forest, aged and
Ageless, stone steps blossomed from
Pure soil. The latch they made of rough
Rope and a hard block of wood, calling
For no key but nimble fingers.

On the day the loose raisins appeared in
The bedclothes, they left a note of welcome,
And the latch unchanged. Asked only that
Paradise be tended as such, a berth unsoiled,
A land unspoiled.

They built a cabin, near the woods
At the back of their land, of lumber
Cut and shaped with bare hands.
A candle, a table, a bed beneath a
Canopy of constellations. They did not own it.

Your Current GPS Location
Jason Ryberg

She tried to tell me that the past
could be simply abandoned like
unclaimed baggage at the airport
or bus station,

or even, one day, with the closing
of a door and the turning of a key—

left behind forever in the rear-view mirror
like a house full of someone else's belongings
(not yours, not anymore) in a town
full of strangers.

But, I say the past can slip
a microchip on you
when you're not looking;

I say the past always knows
your current GPS location.

LET US PRAY
reb

let us pray: bow your heads:

my head is over my knees: metallic air: rust: dust: blood:

mother left in april: for san antonio: hail mary: hail rains:

i am double buckled in the backseat: of a truck: inches away from being swept: into a flood: this town will later remember as: *fierce*:

I used to live in the Cowboy Capital of the World: wake up with ladybugs all over the pillow:

our grief: our downpour: stickers in our bare feet:

ford escape escapees:

grandma sends me a chain email about loving god: how reading the bible makes satan sick to his stomach:

we float to the end of the river and hot asphalt burns our feet until they swell and blister:

there is no other way back:

there is no other way:

to return to the mouth:

POTS & PANS
Zack Kopp

The nt. is cold & flesh is sold   in galleries just down the road

    Long spaces of silence are speech   & the stars are knives
   that stab @ your eyes

You stumble home past churches & brick shit-houses
 all the pots & pans hating the buildings they live in

    All the houses are heads   & the windows are eyes
       each house has a different haircut
   @ home,
this is goddam
serious business, lazy
electric red lilies asleep in the window, your eyes
playing tennis w/ stars & light
   in a glass frying pan

     all nt.

Other times it's a joyride,
        exhaust pipes flashing in the sunset —
zoom —

You get there. You have dreams. You love someone.
The only certainty infection w/ illusion. Some people are there. You

try to make plans. It breaks down. You keep going. It hurts.
There are books, statues. It breaks down again. You keep going.
You're the only one there. You're the only thing real.

A storm of light on the plane of time.

A Condition Without Ghosts
Abigail Chabitnoy

I hadn't seen the woman from Chicago in months
though the guy still walked their hulking Labrador.

But this was the city in sickness
and in health, it wasn't polite to impose.

Under what conditions might a sheet by the road
not assume a body? The shroud

stained funereal so near to the point
of some levied labor.

Is there a condition in which a ghost
is not suspected?

Plastic bags trawl the landscape. Stone
beds wait for us to seed.

The clementines congeal into the grapes
shrink past sweetness and affix themselves

in the rot of last month's spinach. Already dust
settles in the bedroom and piss from a recalculating cat

shadows the tile in the study
if you know where to look.

Last week I found a sand dollar with only a small hole

left of center, I reminded myself

even the winged rats had to eat, had to
play some part, so we're told.

Even birds, requiring something solid to alight
have been known to thread the nest with our disposal.

This morning I saw the black spot
my left ovary a cavity

from which my ark had wrested in motion.
But what about the body

that might or might not have been
underneath the sheet?

The condition always the same:

Let me be some manner of ship
or yes, again, a fish

suited to these streets

The Mother Of The Oxford English Dictionary

Allison Maschoff

mother, n.

definition a.

The female parent of a human being; [2]
> as in the one who feeds you with her chest, the one who housed you next to her most sacred innards, the one your eyes search for as you cry.

a woman in relation to a child or children to whom she has given birth; [3]
> the unparalleled truth of motherhood: only one person will ever birth you.
>
> the unbearable truth of motherhood: no world she births you into will as be as safe as the one she made.

(also in extended use) a woman who undertakes the responsibilities of a parent toward a child [4]
> every place that has ever felt like a second home to me has had the influence of a woman who houses the strength and presence of a whirlwind framing everything from the door to the walls to my heart.

[2] [3] [4] from the Oxford English Dictionary

House of my Heart
Taylor Jones

I'm airing out the house of my heart.
All the cobwebbed corners,
the shelves of knickknacks,
are being dusted
unmercifully.
I'm opening the shutters
letting the wind blow out
the musty smell of disuse.
I'm putting flowers
in all the rooms.
Even the basement, the attic
ignored for so long
are getting a going over.
All that old junk has got to go.
It's just shelter for spiders
that tap away when the lights
come on.

I'm trying to put the house of
my heart in order.
"Smarten up," I say,
adjusting the bowties of my fears.
"Stand up straight," I say,
brushing off the jackets of my doubts.
"Everyone be on your best behavior,"
I say to my wants and needs.
"We have a guest coming."

Tell It Slant
Cortney Collins

My family grew corn in the heartland, but I've never seen it quite like this:

Angelic, husk-winged, guarding every shard of bone hidden in the soil.

How is it that I didn't know I had thousands of angels? They were with me all the time.

I remember going out into the fields with my grandpa, crossing into the humid network, stalks sending out messages to each other across droplets of August air.

I could hear their choir, their low and incandescent hum, the sway of bass clef notes rocking me to sleep in the farmhouse.

Emily Dickenson advised us all to tell the truth slant, and I remember this is what hailstorms taught the fields. The slant truth seemed tragic, in a way, as if nothing stays upright or rooted for long. Not even cornstalks.

Not even families.

Not even farmhouses, burned to the ground long after they've become vacant, when the small town fire department needs a fire to practice on.

Something is always missing.

Maybe it's just a three-hundred-sixty-degree view, the ability to see that everything is overflowing,

all the time.

House of Blues
Susan Carman

She eyes the tired roadhouse
tucked between junk yards filled
with car doors and still-good hubcaps,

hickory smoke heavy on night air,
rubbing against her like a cat.
Inside, past shadowy booths

grimy with time, guitars draw her in
with a walkin' blues line,
shuffle through 12 bars like they mean it.

Ya feelin' blue? the drummer growls,
and the crowd spills onto the dance floor
where she joins women with tight jeans

and tight smiles, moving alone, faces painted
hopeful. When the tune slows,
she takes the hand of a sad-eyed guy—

they slide and sway, his breath
on her neck a sweet refrain
in a song of love gone wrong.

Carved Into Home
Hayden Dansky

I tried on thirteen houses,
five cities,
seven identities,
eight drugs,
three names,
two pronouns, and
two bodies
before I found home.

It didn't matter
where I ran or
even the pace of my step—
The past was always catching up.

It didn't matter
who I wanted
to be—
Shame was my name.
Secrets, my disposition.
Pride, my fantasy.

Words make worlds—[5]
Someone wrapped "they" in a package
with a bow and a card,
put "transgender" in a love note,
tucked "non-binary" in my jacket pocket
when I was passed
out in the corner
of a strangers kitchen,

drunk off
begging my body
to change.

I never knew I could dwell
in my own skin
until I made it mine—
Cleansed it from necessary poison,
injected it with hope,
sculpted it into future,
carved it into home.

[5] From Dominique Christina

Moonlit Slabs of Lights on a Hernandez Church Floor
    Crisosto Apache

a cemetery
                is lit by the light
            of the moon, while time
        stands seemingly still,
     lamenting a
timeless value,
which covers the empty floor
     in a shape
           of a dying face,
the hollow bell knells solemnly
        for the dead to linger there,
     to be buried again
hollering is the reason for
                the isolation of solidarity—
            a tragedy
that befell the dead,
     the decaying reason has taken their chance
beneath a standing tree made into crosses,
the mountains are alive
              yet they appear dead,
        there is no willful purpose,
while a fly sits humming on the sill
     and ants gather,
to confirm the time is still ticking,
that light gleaming on the floorboards,
never ends the ceasing shadow   —but it does

—but that light
   is beyond the dead

A POEM WHICH MAY BE MISTAKEN FOR THE THANK YOU LETTER I READ OUT LOUD TO THE FUNDERS OF THE PRESTIGIOUS FELLOWSHIP I WON LAST SUMMER, A FELLOWSHIP WHICH DID ABSOLUTELY FUCK ALL TO SAVE MY AUTISTIC BLACK MUSLIM BODY FROM BEING INTERROGATED BY THOSE CBP/TSA TERRORISTS AT THE AIRPORT

Said Shaiye

- It strikes me as odd that this school, this fellowship, has no protocols in place for students that are forcibly interrogated at the border. I guess I shouldn't expect much from an institution, and I guess I should bite my tongue and do the polite thing, talk about how amazing my trip was. But my trip was not amazing. It was fraught, painful, nerve-wracking. I was sick from the moment I got there to the moment I left. I walked into all types of bureaucratic walls—people not believing I was actually there to do research, and so forth. Worst of all, when I needed medical help, I had to pay out of pocket because the insurance was a formality. Oh sure, they reimbursed me for the expenses, but only partially. The idea of a medical evacuation was dangled before me, but I quickly lost hope in that. I was sick to my stomach the day I boarded my return flight, cutting my trip a full month short. Besides pain, all I had on my mind was TSA/CBP. Would they harass me? Where is home for someone like me? I am an Autistic Somali Man traveling from Kenya—that's a perfect terrorist profile I fit. 20 Some hours later, I arrived in the states. They ask me pedantic questions about my research and MN Nice me with "good for you." They do all this as they shuffle me into a tertiary screening line, confronted by lazy feds with mustard stains on their plaid shirts. I know what questions they want to ask me, because I've seen this movie before. But I refuse to answer their questions. I watch the older Somali man – the only other person asked to go to this special line before we can leave the airport – duck his head and smile and comply with their hellacious line of questioning. I stand my ground like a Zimmerman defense. But I am also weak. I can barely stand. They threaten to go through my luggage down to the underwear. To confiscate my devices and see who I've been talking to. We can do this the easy way or the hard way, they tell me. I can feel my heartbeat racing every time I recall this memory. There are no words to describe how livid I was when I finally got home—after answering their stupid questions, knowing I had no choice, feeling like a failure for acquiescing. I emailed my contacts at the university, both in my department and at the fellowship. There were a bunch of emails back and forth, a lot of concern and apologizing, but I knew nothing would come of it. I knew I would not see justice, just as I knew I was labeled a terrorist from a piece of shit country the moment I was born. I reached out to CAIR, the ACLU, filed formal complaints with CBP. Nothing nothing nothing came of any of it. All of this reinforced the idea that my life is worthless. Absolutely meaningless. And that is why I do the work I do, write the way I do, and live the way I do. I have no choice. I wish I could say I'll be applying for this fellowship again. I have no reason to. And if I could go back in time, I wouldn't have applied in the first place. Thanks for your time.

*Author's Note: All of this really happened, from the events in the poem, to my reading this to the people who partially funded my trip. I was supposed to be more grateful, I guess? Funny, I've never felt good about thanking white people for anything, least of all a few measly dollars. Sometimes poems are all we have to cuss people out with. And if they wanna cuss back, well, I guess they'll have to learn how to write poetry first. That's a joke. Laugh.

A Special Place
Norbert Góra

There is no such
second place in the world
where so many noteworthy
moments have been saved.
How many of your breaths
flickered on the walls,
how many of your tears
soaked the floor,
nobody knows.
A part of your heart
will stay here forever,
no matter where
the wings of fate take you.
It's a magic point,
the mind remembers it
as the heart long for it,
one and only—home.

Floor Bare
Jessica Rigney

And here you are standing
two feet bare on the floor of
your kitchen turning back
to the wall behind as though
he were standing bare-footed there
with you again as he did
those years prior. Before
the days dissolved into the rising
of time immemorial and you
who had just kept your head
above water now live
in the after so far below you have
come to know the nocturnal
creatures who in quiet habits roam
from shore to shore only under
all the weight of dark stars.
What can you do but let
flow through your fingers—the now
and him too though he was yours
for a time and gave you
such happiness.
The distances between
keep widening and soon it will be
that you cannot recall his eyes
or the scent amongst his thick curls.
Turns out you knew—had known
all along this was coming. It was why
you held him close for so long
why you saved him in dreams

so many times you lost count. It was
the one sure thing you held
in your heart and though you knew
it to be true you gave him
everything even so—even though
you knew in the coming years
he would be gone from you.
And here you are standing
two feet bare on the floor of
your kitchen turning back
to the wall behind you as though
he were standing bare-footed there.

Lean Home
Jessica Rigney

After the locusts devour our crops
And the geese lay down to rest on the remains

There you sit with crushed wheat beneath. Your
White shirt trembles against a turquoise sky.

Dew light rises from the field. Grackles call
From the osage flocked full—a shift of darkness

By a thousand wings. You say cormorant
Cormorant in formulaic repetition though

We reside on a prairie far from any sea.
I sit down beside you—ink blue.

We've forfeited the baby this time
Through no fault of our own. I say.

I'll bury what passes in the kitchen garden
With what's left of the creeping thyme. Then we are

Quiet in the slow rustle of a lowing wind. And we lean
Into one another as home—as we will again.

We are lost. Save for what is slow to be known
Of calm and hope and the tides of crops and wings.

Progress, Mexico
Dustin King

1.

The stray dogs bite. There's glass in the sand,
too worn to cut a toe. A toddler giggles
running from her family toward the
waves. They urge her back. On the beach
road, I can't tell if the sound of a car
approaching from behind is the surf until
headlights flash. The gate of the abandoned
school for "incapacitados" is chained shut,
has been for months, sargassum and plastic
washing under. Classroom walls of cracked
concrete. Graffiti on graffiti. A phantom yell
of *gringo*! Spitting rain. It will pour any minute.
Then it doesn't. The yacht club sells pizzas
to expats but no one is hungry tonight. Wind
scatters plastic chairs around tables as if
customers were full and anxious to get
home, then as if the patio were raided by
stray dogs. Each palm tree has a personal
hair dryer. The expats, like stray dogs,
growl at newcomers, bark at each other
into the night. The expats feed the stray dogs.
Cheapest alarm system I ever had, says
one to another. A pack gathers in front of
his second home like hyenas, vicious, grinning.
Testicles, teats, purpled, withered fruit clinging
to the vine. They shit where they want. A passerby
steps in it, curses. A passerby kicks out but
we see who is really afraid. A passing car

accelerates, achieves revenge. The corpse
of a stray dog in a ditch stinking until
it won't anymore. Expats think the pandemic
a hoax or conspiracy initiated by Jews.
The expats are assholes, says an expat, *but
they are old. They die quick.* One, on his
moto, was run over by a microbus last week.
He exploded like a McDonalds ketchup package.

    2.
I speak to a loved one on the phone. She
insists, *there is something you're not telling me.*
Twists and flecks of iridium, extraterrestrial
metal, shocked quartz and glass beads discovered
in the rock core. Water-winged children hurling
themselves into cenotes, earth's empty eye sockets,
prehispanic graveyards, skeletons fished
out from 100 meters deep, bats zig-zagging
over water underground. I'm alone in the
port city of Progreso. Chicxclub, site of
climate disruption, mass extinction, ancient
rerouting of life. A meteor with the power of
1,000 atomic bombs. We won't give the
universe time for another go. A seagull missing
a foot lands near my dinner, gingerly using the
stump for balance, swaying more than usual in
the breeze. A flamingo limping across a salty lake.
A stray dog hopping. An ex-pat in a wheelchair.
Landmine in Afghanistan. Crowded hovels
with no running water inland. Abandoned
mansions on the coast. Mold, erosion,
dilapidation. A hurricane isn't at fault.
The money ran out or virus. Crackling bass

and reggaetón and shouts from inside one
shell of a building that isn't theirs, the
windows boarded up and papered over.
From the terrace three floors up a young
Mexican points to the liter of beer in his hand
and yells, ¡Súbate, Güero! I pass through a door
with a busted lock.

    3.
A group of 20-somethings chugging beer
around an empty pool. Racing to
inebriation. Pulling ahead in the race to
elude annihilation. Assembled from various
regions of Mexico, here to construct a suburbia
of sorts outside the port city, an international
village. They pass me a joint, I bum them
English cigarettes too expensive for Mexico.
They push a phone with a PowerPoint
presentation in front of me. Condos with
rooftop gardens, windmills, and solar panels
resembling Mayan pyramids constructed over
the ruins of Mayan pyramids long ago
chewed, swallowed, and still being digested by
jungle. Graphene super metal and recycled
plastics. Bubble tech and defoaming. Optimum
insulation and acoustics, less CO2 release. Jargon,
gospel, babble of sustainability. New lingo for
the industry, the lexicon, the public imagination.
Off the grid. Supposedly free from the control
and corruption of government, of cartels. I say it
sounds like a cult and an interior designer giggles
wiggling her pointer finger up and down, says
sí, sí, como Charley Manson. Voice automated

everything—your entertainment, your coffee
pot, your bidet. All-inclusive. More amenities
promised than a liberal arts college. A Burger
King. Probably a mini-Target. The promise
of consumerism preserved amid the crash
of exterior markets. Top priority: Security.
AK-47s, M-16s, Uzis. Bulletproof vests and
jackets that look like you're going to church
or brunch. Fences with barbed wire as tall
as border walls. Here in the shell of an ex-expat's
vacation home the other American dream of
the gated community lifted, romanticized,
enhanced. Ultra-militarized. *Elon Musk might
support the project,* claims an energy specialist.
Living there will be like working for Google,
boasts the jungle rave DJ. *There is opportunity
in crisis,* they add. They have acquired the land.
Started construction. Convinced expats to invest,
possibly retire there. I jokingly ask the CEO, *Who
will be eaten first when the apocalypse comes?*
He nods toward a stray dog eying us from below
and as serious as climate change says,
could be any of us.

The Old Homestead
M. Palowski Moore

Perched on borrowed
Bricks and mortar
Are seven rooms;
Four large, three small—
walls of weathered wood
Where grandpa's heart,
Precious menagerie
Of memories,
No longer remains.
Grandma's gone and the city
Owns the house now.

Old pa's grandmother, a slave,
Died here. His father, a sharecropper
With fist like stone, farmed this land
'Till he and the plow gave out.
His mother, who nurtured and fed
Thirteen children and cried at
The cold, pot-bellied stove when
Three died in the sweep
Of the great depression
She, too, passed in this place.

Across the meadow
Where pecan trees towered
When cotton was king
The train passed this place-
Twice during the day
Once at night.

Now, the tracks
Are rust and overgrown,
The depot a departure
Long lost, forgotten.

City planners, officials,
Businessmen hatch ruin—
Eggs like
The boll weevil laid
Long ago
In my grandparents' fields—
A consuming hunger
That toiled and turned
The promise of harvest
Rotten and rust brown.

Soon there will be a highway
To spirit travelers to and fro:
Places, people: shopping, speeding
Towards modernity while
Robots pass by;
Marching, marking time
Rising, replacing
Traces of history.

Today, the cotton is high
Beneath cirrus clouds
Of shadows crossing
Floating, covering
A street once lined by
Elms, firs, oaks and honeysuckle
Still stands the Old Homestead
A cradle of comfort

Soon to be paved clean
For the latest progress
A nod to the relentless spirit
Of advancing, displacing, erasing.

Delayed Homecoming
Jayati Das

There are quite a few miles that crevice you from home,

Like the zip of your suitcase that flies between hope and

not-hope.

I can only imagine how the fridge door must be slamming,

unlike the one back here—

Extended supplies shunting faster than Turner's baby,

The one that cries but never comes.

Do you wake each day to a finite line

And trace back the rhino's trail

You had smiled about the other day?

Does Bishop speak clearer now

And blur your vocabulary?

I am afraid I will forget your smiling hair

And the exact shade of your red lipstick

(The traces are already starting to drift).

Lie to me when I ask about happiness

Or perhaps halt the track of my question

('Are you home yet?')

With a whistle or a red flag,

For then I can at least begin to unmemorise

Your face greeting me in some departure lounge.

Suburban Mandala
Boyd Bauman

Om of the lawnmower motor,
the meditative motion begins,
this tracing of the sacred square.

Castes least enlightened outsource,
content to admire aesthetics from afar.
The devout deny such urges,
don robes of an ancestral order:
button down western shirts,
before mounting mini John Deeres,
while those nearest nirvana self-propel,
lean step by measured step into each swath
as if laying down something native
on a Kansas prairie.

Cut grass like incense
awakens the senses.

Emptying themselves of the envy within
the outward gaze across the fence,
these Midwestern monks
are quite conscious of their lot,
rectangular orbits mere representations
of the workings and wonder
of the cosmos.

Prostration is sometimes required,
negotiating with the earth
over weeds noxious, obnoxious,

other blessed imperfections.

A single blade clings to the sweat
on an arm,
the rest released to the currents
of June rain or a.m. sprinklers,
the mandala regenerating perpetually.

Each steward inhales,
exhales,
accepting this perfection
ephemeral,
embracing this transience and a want
for nothing.

The House We Build Together
Cristopher Clauss

I do not ask her
if she believes
that the fairies will really come,
that they might be searching for a tiny backyard house
in which to dwell.
Even if they were,
no magical creature would choose
to live in this tangle of sticks
over which we have fussed
for far too long.
It doesn't matter
that the bed of moss
will go un-slept in.
I will not worry myself
with exactness or proportions
of bark chair to mushroom table.
The fairies will never complain
about such things.
We busy ourselves
with flower petal carpets
and arranging decorations
of shiny quartz pebble just so.
The final product
is never quite what she envisioned.
The furnishings are rustic
and the roof keeps falling in
each time it is adjusted

by little fingers with the best of intentions.
She will remember
building everything herself.
When it is gone,
when the rain
and breeze
and rot have scattered the remnants
she will remember it
as a jeweled palace,
a luxurious home.
She will sleep comfortably
in her own bed
knowing the fairies
are well cared for,
imagining she had tucked them in herself,
kissed them gently on the forehead
the way Daddy does
before he whispers
good night.

I Am Trying to Remember if I Married For Love
Kimberly Ann Priest

Long beams are carried in on strong arms,
belts fitted with tools and the Oklahoma sun
warming the backs of the heads of workers
remodeling the house across the street
though it's colder than usual for these parts
in February—even a dusting of snow. The grass
crunches beneath their boots, dry, and blonde
like a young woman's hair, as I watch them
unload their truck, turning toward one another
now and then to chat or chuckle or pat a back
before lifting another board. The windows
of this home must be original, the same panes
of glass it was born with and I wonder
if they will be replaced, if the paper that surely
continues to adorn the walls, peeling,
will be stripped, its bones re-fleshed in fresher
hues, if the organs that pump life into toilets,
showers, and sinks, into outlets, lights,
hairdryers, and phones will undergo surgery.
How long until the porch is secure
and the roof healed of all its leaking? A few
bi-fold doors lean against the home's old siding—
closets, it seems, have been opened and rendered
doorless as heaps of a former life are gathered
in piles of trash that exit the home in large bags.
Down the street at the halfway house,
men smoking cigarettes also observe

this pageantry with me and I wonder if they
are thinking what I am thinking—that someone
bought that house with all its imperfections,
after an assessment, not knowing exactly
how the whole thing will turn out. The sky
grows overcast and snow begins to fall again
so the men at the halfway house drop embers
unto the sidewalk to go indoors
as the workers hood their heads and continue
working. I pull my blanket tighter over
my shoulders letting the cool flakes fall against
my face and litter the doorstep around me.
I can't leave now no matter what happens—
this is the part of the story I still like.

August A Place
Lori Brack

The front was sand and yellow wheat and brown horseflesh and night whistle of a train. The back was a gate unlatched onto summer – flower patches and sprinklers, blue television windows floating in the dark. Before builders poured foundations down the block, I ran there between rows of corn. Sunsets blazed or whispered and disappeared past railroad tracks at the horizon, the distance I could figure going under my own steam, the faraway I imagined growing up to find.

Moving Through
Wheeler Light

the uncertain shape
of places we lived

I am writing
in the present

and ending up
in the past:

the kitchen island—
sofa and coffee table

was the room for the family
or the living? Our dog

skips and tackles
a memory of you

to the ground and licks
its face. You shouted

Winston, Off
though there's nowhere

I'd rather be than
tackled eternally

by our big dog
too insane to take

after you died.
Your father called me

and told me
I could have Winston

and every poem lately
begins like this—

wanting one thing
and getting another

and so I want to write
about places we lived

and I want to write about you
but am left with a dog instead

your poetry lining the walls
of our bedroom, bathroom,

walk-in closet full of ghost clothes
your ghost body slips into perfectly

inhabiting the space between
believing and longing

which I know
is uninhabitable but keeps

coming back as though
a dog with whom I am playing fetch.

You wrote *wake from a fever-dream*
to a dog's yelp and so I wake up

drenched in memory
with your name always

echoing off this apartment's walls.

The Idukki Dam
Anu Lal

The British built it, upon our home,
In Idukki*, amidst the feral mountains
Of Western Ghats**,
This structure—a leviathan of construction,
Which they said was
The symbol of modernity,
An accomplishment of human effort,
This sterile, dark, tearing off the heart,
Of the Western Ghats,
The dam with which they also ruled,
Nature with alacrity.
For two hundred years, the empire governed
Our desires and hopes, destinies and dreams.
Our home enchained,
Under the hoof of the emperor's horse,
Dying, rising, dying again, rising again,
Like an old creature heaving for its last breath.
But the old and spent
Doesn't impress the empire,
And it left this land, its nature,
And the people, with a tale
Of condescending kindness,
Letting the "young" nation self-govern,
With warnings of possible schisms.
But with general consolations
At the possible victories gained:
Like the railways, the dams, the roads,
And the democratic spirit.
The siren of the train is bearable,

And so is the sluggishness
Of the democratic system,
And bureaucracy, but the dam—
A silent monstrosity of Idukki,
Governing the Ghats with its grey bosom,
Serving mostly electric power-supplies.
It's old, with dark lines of age growing
On the ramparts of the reservoirs,
Mossy, slippery wall, waiting—
For its final fall, every Monsoon,
Drowning our dwelling places
Underneath the dammed up spirit
Of the wild and tortured river,
Surpassing human alacrity.
So when the rains ravage,
We hear the echoes, of death—
Riding the horse of the old emperor,
Upon the ramparts of the old walls,
With the fear of death,
Still governing us.

[6] Idukki is one of the southern restrictions in Kerala state, India, which is situated in the Western Ghats. [7] Western Ghats is a chain of mountains bordering Kerala's western side, which is known as ecologically fragile.

Days of Red and Gold
David Estringel

Sittin' at the kitchen table—cup of black coffee in one hand, cigarette in the other—I look past catches of blue paint and the remains of flies on screen door mesh, toward the sorghum field just beyond the ranch gate. Death's stillness—a gravity all its own—has seeped into every corner, permeated the grout of tiled countertops and spaces in between fruit magnates on the old, white Frigidaire like the smell of rabbit in the oven or hints of storm riding out on the breeze. Life's left the room—no pulse under these linoleum tiles—it seems, leaving it darker, a bit colder, despite morning's come to call through the window above the sink. I take another sip—bitter on the tongue—then a drag (or two), finding myself—absent-minded--fingering the contents of a chipped, pink and white bowl of green stamp china (of which she was so proud). *Four pennies, two dimes, and a nickel. Two rusty paper clips. A half-used packet of B&C headache powder. A dead fly.* I remember eating from it—sweetened raspberries, red and golden, from bushes in the garden—when I was small. How I'd toss them back in grubby fistfuls, between chokes on the juice, as honied explosions—sour and sweet—took me to Heaven and back then 'round, again, while she looked out the screen door, tossing hair from her eyes—cup of black coffee in one hand, cigarette in the other—staring at my father working in the field, beyond.

Missing her, I think how lovely it was when all you needed to attack the day was a belly full of hunger and a spoonful of sugar (or two).

WHERE WILL WE DWELL?
Destiny Armstrong

After you move from a home,
No one will ever know the memories it held.
Like the laughter that filled the dining room every night at dinner.
The Christmas tree that went up and down.
Like a roller coaster year after year after year.
They won't know the room that held you after every loss,
Or break up or days when you just didn't want to wake up.
They won't know the wedding you held in your backyard for your children.
You see, all of this and more will become erased behind the white paint they overlay that marked the heights of your grandchildren.
It will all fade away making room for new memories.
Yet the house will know your history.
And although the house will never know why you left,
It will embrace a new family with a new chapter to start.

PORTRAIT OF A BEDROOM WALL
Andrew Walker

We do not push the walls out
but instead pull the room in, drink
our already small space. My clothes,
washed and bagged, are still too big
for this disappearing body—it's like
a magic trick: blink and you'll miss
me. I'm not tangible anymore, these
bed bugs eating away more than just
our bedspread. Touch this translucent skin
and maybe you'll find something
stronger than the body I see before me
in tinted windows, in tagged pictures.
I think about *House of Leaves*, the home
that did not know what size it was,
about the men who found themselves
less than they thought they knew, the codes
hidden, dark filled with whatever meaning
the reader can pour from themselves

> I mistakenly called this place a home.
> I walled myself in,
> there are no doors here
> this is not an entrance.

HOME
Caleb Ferganchick

Growing up, my home was a closet. Not the metaphorical closet where I tucked my sexuality. More precisely, my home was an 8x11in guide to Colorado fish my grandfather gave me to mold my sexuality. Which I tucked inside my closet. In which were tucked letters to my adolescent loves like Jamie, Ally, Shelly, and Jack (especially to Jack). In which, I dreamed of our skeletal home without closets. Where my mother did not tuck her guilt, and the father did not tuck his abusive addictions. Where Jack drove the Hot Wheels car he gave me after our play date. Just like Ken in Aqua's Barbie Doll.

There is no instruction manual with the postscript delivered by the owl to your closet proclaiming, "You're a homosexual, Harry." By trial and error, you come to understand the fragility of home. And the fragility of queer. And how both must often be constructed like lean-tos on the pull-out couches of allies.

Like tornados, like earthquakes, like tsunamis, like men in I.C.E. uniforms, my nature was a disaster a home could not weather. So, home became a lonely rainbow. A refraction of tears staining pictures of cutthroat trout.

Whether by cosmic dramatic irony or systematic oppression, when your home is queer, so often your home becomes a bar. Where fags bundle like fags. And smoke fags. And drink like, well, like fish. Most of whom are obsessed with being fish. So, I learned a new language that gave transformative space to my transient home. Sashay! Shontay! Cinched! Boots the house down! Beat for the gods!

I learned that language, too, was a home. Ours was one that could not be deciphered. Because no one cares to decipher why our family struggles with substance abuse at nearly twice the average rate. How our expansive forest of intersectional trees denoting our lineage drinks from a stigmatized watering hole. Yet, the branches stay sturdy enough for us to take our lives at five times the average rate.

I have read enough obituaries to know how mine may sound. *Taken unexpectedly. After a long struggle.* As if the struggle was never an indication of the homophobe. Or the revolver. Or how unsurprisingly often they're the same. I mean, the gay homophobe with a revolver. Taking a family with him that would have died to show him how to live. In a home called queer.
I will be survived by a long list of family that never embraced me. With no mention of the love that allowed me to survive.

But I have found home.

My home is not a structure I ride shotgun to in Jack's hot wheel car. Home is not a bed on which I lay my head when the world insists I don't belong. My home cannot be taken by a natural or xenophobic disaster. Home is not a mortality statistic. My home is not an early grave.

My home is queer.

And I vow my home will always be open to anyone who thinks theirs is just a closet filled with unread love letters.

House Song
Aerik Francis

As the hearth of the home—yours—
the heart. The house echoes, hollow.
I hear quiet louder. Absent

your noise, I hear the aging floors—
Earth's ground shifting. I'm sifting through
Earth's silt, the rubble that follows.

Hollow rumbling heartbeat—absent—
I hear your pulse echoing through.

Poet Bios

Wheeler Light is an MFA candidate at the University of Virginia. His work has appeared or is forthcoming in *Hobart*, *Pretty Owl Poetry*, *The Penn Review*, and *Broadsided Press*, among others. His work can be found at www.wheelerlight.net

Liza Sparks (she/her) is an intersectional feminist, writer, poet, and creative. She is a brown-multiracial-queer-woman living and working in Colorado. Her work has appeared with *Ghost City Review*, *Bozalta Collective*, *Cosmonauts Avenue*, and many others; and is forthcoming with *Honey Literary*, Split This Rock's social justice database—*The Quarry*, and will be included in *Nonwhite and Woman Anthology* published by Woodhall Press in 2022. Liza was a semifinalist for Button Poetry's Chapbook contest in 2018 and was a finalist for Denver Lighthouse Writers Workshop Emerging Writer Fellowship in Poetry in 2020 and 2019. She is a poetry reader for *The Chestnut Review*. You can read more of Liza's work at lizasparks.com, IG @sparksliza534, or TW @lizathepoet.

M. Palowski Moore is a poet, writer, and storyteller. He has five volumes of poetry, including the Lambda Award nominee *BURNING BLUE*. His compositions reflect diverse themes and interpretations of prejudice, racism, socioeconomic inequality, homophobia, and systemic oppression. He is a contributing poet to the Civil Rights Memorial Center (SPLC) community poem *A CIVIL COMMUNITY*, a new exhibit that will be featured inside the final gallery of The Civil Rights Memorial Center.

Caleb Ferganchick is a rural, queer, slam poet activist and author of *Poetry Heels* (2018). His work has been featured and published by the *South Broadway Ghost Society* (2020, 2021), "Slam Ur Ex ((the podcast))" (2020), and *The Colorado Mesa University Literary Review*. He organizes the annual "Slamming Bricks" poetry slam competition in honor of the 1969 Stonewall Riots and serves as a board member to Western Colorado Writer's Form. A SUP river guide, Caleb also dreams of establishing a queer commune with a river otter rescue and falconry. He lives in Grand Junction, Colorado.

Jade Lascelles is a writer, editor, musician, and letterpress printer based in Boulder, Colorado. She is the author of the full-length collection *The Invevitable* (Gesture Press, 2021). Selections of her work have also appeared in numerous journals and the anthologies *Women of Resistance: Poems for a New Feminism* and *Precipice: Writing at the Edge*, as well as being featured in the Ed Bowes film Gold Hill and the visual art exhibit and accompanying book Shame Radiant. Several of her poems were recently translated into Italian for the journal *Le Voci della Luna*. Beyond her writing endeavors, she is a longtime steward of the Harry Smith Print Shop at Naropa University, a core member of the art group The Wilds, and plays drums in a few different musical projects.

Lillian Fuglei is a Colorado based poet. She began writing poetry in High School, after a lifetime of attending open mics thanks to her mother. She currently bounces between two of the highest paying jobs possible, substitute teaching and freelance journalism. You can find her on Instagram at @literary.lillian.

Jozer G is a poet musician and actor based out of Denver, Colorado! Jozer's work has been featured on American Theater Magazine, HBO, PBS and Univision. Jozer is set to release his debut EP on June 24th, and a new book at the end of the year!

Liam Max Kelley is a Chilean-American playwright, actor, poet, and high school language arts teacher. He is the program director at Stain'd Arts, an arts non-profit based in Denver, Colorado, and the co-founder of RuddyDuck Theatre Company, a local absurdist theatre group. He writes poetry to avoid making an argument, to highlight life's horrid ambiguities, and to turn the heads of those he holds dear.

Rue Kream is a writer and photographer in Southeastern Massachusetts. Her work has appeared in *Home Education Magazine, Life Learning Magazine, Connections,* and *The Natural Child Project*.

When not writing poems, **Jason Ryberg** can often be found enjoying an adult beverage while sitting in the healing waters of the Gasconade River, just outside of Belle, MO. If you would like to visit sometime, you may contact him at chile66046@yahoo.com. Be advised that there are snakes and lizards and, apparently, at least one bear sighting. Wait, what!?

Abigail Chabitnoy, member of the Tangirnaq Native Village in Kodiak, is the author of *How to Dress a* Fish (Wesleyan 2019), shortlisted for the 2020 International Griffin Prize for Poetry and winner of the 2020 Colorado Book Award, and the linocut illustrated chapbook *Converging Lines of Light* (Flower Press 2021). Her poems have appeared in *Hayden's Ferry Review, Boston Review, Tin House, Gulf Coast, LitHub,* and *Red Ink,* among others. She currently teaches at the Institute of American Indian Arts and Eastern Oregon University low-residency MFA programs as well as Lighthouse in Denver. Find her at salmonfisherpoet.com.

Allison Maschhoff is a creative writing MFA student at the University of Missouri, Kansas City. Her poetry has been published in *The Blue Route, Green Blotter, Windfall,* and *Better Than Starbucks*. She also writes fiction. You can find links to her work at www.allisonmaschhoff.com or follow @allison.maschhoff on Instagram.

Taylor Jones' fiction and poetry has appeared in *Spit Poet Zine, Smoky Quartz, South Broadway Ghost Society,* and *Barren Magazine.* Her website is: tjonesportfolio.wixsite.com/taylorjones. She was born and raised on the East Coast, but now lives in Denver, Colorado, in a house full of plants.
Twitter: @I_heart_fungi.
Insta: @tjonespainting

Zack Kopp is a freelance writer, editor, photographer, graphic artist, and literary agent currently living in Denver, Colorado. His informal history of the Beat Generation's connections with Denver was published by The History Press in 2015. Kopp's books are available at Amazon, and you can find his blog at the website for his indie hybrid press at www.campelasticity.com featuring interviews and articles and links to other websites. His improvised novel, *Public Hair,* was described by one critic as "simultaneously the best and worst book ever." The latest chapter of Kopp's "fantastic biography" (Cf. Billy Childish), *Henry Crank's History of Wonders* is expected in 2022.

reb (she/they) is not a girl but is a horse girl. their heart is on fire!

Cortney Collins lives on the Front Range of Colorado with her two beloved feline companions, Pablo (after Neruda) and Lida Rose (after a barbershop quartet song in The Music Man). She is the founder of the pandemic-era virtual poetry open mic, Zoem. Zoem produced an anthology of its poets' work, Magpies: A Zoem Anthology, of which she is co-editor. Her work has been published by South Broadway Press, 24hr Neon Mag, Amethyst Magazine, Sheila-na-Gig, Back Patio Press, and others. Cortney considers herself a poet secondarily; her first calling is encouraging others' beautiful words in community. My IG: @wordsaretheuniverse

Jessica Rigney is a poet, artist, and filmmaker. She lives and wanders in Colorado and northern New Mexico, where she films and collects feathers and stones. www.jessicarigney.com

Susan Carman is a Pushcart Prize nominee, and served as poetry editor for Kansas City Voices. Her poetry appeared most recently in I-70 Review, Heartland! Poetry of Love, Resistance & Solidarity, and the anthologies Curating Home and The Shining Years. Retired from non-profit management, she lives in Overland Park, Kansas, where she is an ESL volunteer.

Norbert Góra is a 31 years old poet and writer from Poland. He is the author of more than 100 poems which have been published in poetry anthologies in USA, UK, India, Nigeria, Kenya and Australia.

Hayden Dansky (pronouns: they/them/theirs) is a nonbinary rural queer kid trying their best to not to be smothered by capitalism. They have been writing and performing poetry for several years, and are currently collaborating with local experimental musicians, dancers, and videographers to create performances that encompass multiple disciplines. They just published their first full length poetry book called *I Would Tell You a Secret*. Their most recent poetry can also be found in anthologies such as *Bible Belt Queers*, *Thought for Food*, South Broadway Ghost Society Online Journal, and *Spit Poet Volume 8*. They are also the Executive Director of Boulder Food Rescue, a nonprofit working to create a more just and less wasteful food system, through the sustainable redistribution of healthy food and participatory and community-led food access systems. Instagram: @haydendansky haydendansky.com

Crisosto Apache is from Mescalero Apache Reservation in New Mexico (US) and lives in Lakewood, CO. They are Mescalero, Chiricahua Apache, and Diné of the Salt Clan born for the Towering House Clan. They are Assistant Professor of English and Associate Poetry Editor for The Offing Magazine. Crisosto's debut collection GENESIS (Lost Alphabet) stems from the vestiges of memory and cultural identity of self-emergence as language, body, and cosmology. Crisosto is an Associate Professor of English at the Rocky Mountain College of Art & Design. They hold an MFA from the Institute of American Indian Arts in Santa Fe, NM.

Said Shaiye is an Autistic Somali writer & photographer from Seattle who now lives in Minneapolis. He is a Disability Storytelling Graduate Assistant with Minnesota Transform. He has published in Pithead Chapel, 580 Split, Entropy, Diagram, Rigorous, and elsewhere. His debut book, Are You Borg Now? (Really Serious Literature, 2021) was named a Minnesota Book Award Finalist in Creative Nonfiction & Memoir. He can be reached at www.saidshaiye.com

Boyd Bauman grew up on a small ranch near Bern, Kansas, his dad the storyteller, mom the family scribe. His books of poetry are Cleave and Scheherazade Plays the Chestnut Tree Café. After stints in New York, Colorado, Alaska, Japan, and Vietnam, Boyd writes in Kansas City.
Visit at boydbauman.weebly.com.

Dustin King teaches Spanish and runs a small organization that provides aid to undocumented community in Richmond, VA. His poems appear in Blood and Bourbon, Ligeia, Tilted House, Drunk Monkey, and other magazines. He most recently made the longlist in the 2021 UK national poetry competition.

Jayati Das is a research scholar from Tezpur University, India, and holds a Master's degrees in English Literature from the University of Delhi. Her areas of research include representations of the Vietnam War, masculinity studies, and queer cinema. She has won over a dozen prizes in creative writing at the college and university levels. Several of her poems and stories have been published in

The Assam Tribune, The Sentinel, and e-magazines like The Golden Line, including a story in an anthology titled DU Love. Her published research includes essays on the Mizo poet, Mona Zote, race in Othello, and on Pedro Almodóvar's cinema.

Christopher Clauss (he/him) is an introvert, Ravenclaw, father, poet, photographer, and middle school science teacher in rural New Hampshire. His mother believes his poetry is "just wonderful." Both of his daughters declare that he is the "best daddy they have," and his pre-teen science students rave that he is "Fine, I guess. Whatever."

Lori Brack is the author of *A Case for the Dead Letter Detective* (Kelsay, 2021), *Museum Made of Breath* (Spartan Kansas City, 2018) and *A Fine Place to See the Sky* (The Field School, 2010). She lives on the prairie two blocks from the Garden of Eden and 14 miles from the geodetic center of North America.

David Estringel is a Xicanx writer with words at *The Opiate, Red Fez,* and *Poetry NI*. He has published two books of poetry, *Indelible Fingerprints* and *Blood Honey*, followed by three poetry chapbooks, *Punctures, PeripherieS,* and *Eating Pears* on the Rooftop. Connect with David on Twitter @The_Booky_Man and www.davidaestringel.com.

Kimberly Ann Priest is the author of *Slaughter the One Bird* (Sundress Publications 2021) as well as chapbooks *The Optimist Shelters in Place* (Harbor Editions 2022), *Parrot Flower* (Glass 2021), *Still Life* (PANK 2020), and *White Goat Black Sheep* (FLP 2018). Winner of the 2019 Heartland Poetry Prize in the *New Poetry from the Midwest* anthology by New American Press, she is currently an Assistant Professor of First-Year Writing at Michigan State University, an associate editor for the *Nimrod International Journal of Prose and Poetry* and the James Tolan Writer in Residence at Writer's House PGH. Find more of her work at kimberlyannpriest.com

Anu Lal is a writer from India. He has written extensively about his homeland, the South Indian State named Kerala. His works include poetry, short stories, novella, novel, and nonfiction. His major works include: *The Notions of Living, The Notions of Healing* (anthologies), *Stories We Live, Thalassery Biryani* (Short story collections) and *Life After the Floods* (nonfiction). Instagram: @authorlal

Destiny Armstrong is a 22-year-old poet living here in Denver Colorado. Home was a concept that seemed foreign to me. I moved homes 3 times in my childhood. Was homeless with my family on and off until I was 6 years old. Found myself homeless again my senior year of high school. Poetry has been my outlet for years. I look back, not to dwell on the past, but to see what I have overcome.

Aerik Francis (they/them/he/him) is a Queer Black & Latinx poet and teaching artist based in Denver, Colorado, USA. They are a Canto Mundo poetry fellow and a The Watering Hole fellow. They are also a poetry reader for *Underblong poetry journal* and an event coordinator for Slam Nuba. They have poetry published widely, links of which may be found at linktr.ee/Aerik or via their website phaentompoet.com . Find them on IG/TW @phaentompoet

Editor Bios

Emylee Frank (she/her) helps the Denver band Saeva write poems to the sky. Emylee also runs her own Astrology/Mystic-themed Instagram, *@eclipselunairee*.

Kali Love Heals loves you. They basically love everyone. Unless you're shitty. Please don't be shitty. They hope to help others find healing and wholeness. They are a multi-genre writer, performer, and activist, and CIO of the sweet tech startup #lovework, helping teams love their work so they can love their lives. They have created ritual, dance, and theater works with *The Shamanic Dolls, Crescent Dance Project,* and in *The Ballet of Masculine and Feminine Divinities*. They have toured with their music and poetry as *Many Medicines* and the Denver funk band *The Pamlico Sound*. Kali is editor here at South Broadway Press, and their contributions have included *Queen City Companion, Punketry, Jazzetry, Howl at the Moon, Unpact,* our last lovely book, *Thought for Food,* and more. Through their work and writing on their concept of *Communitive Justice*, they are committed to supporting community education, expression, and building better systems through conflict resolution. They are currently focused on #lovework and the intersections of biotech, individual and group success, flow states, and life satisfaction. Mostly, they hope you all enjoy your choices. *@kaliheals @manymedicines*

Terra Iverson is thrilled to be on the South Broadway Press editing team. Originally a businesswoman, her passion has always been in the written word. Ink is an art form, painting your world in the minds of others. The meaning of a word, the structure of a stanza, the moment when you forget who you are because it is all so powerful. Terra loves those moments. She's often found reading nearly everywhere she goes, even while walking, which she doesn't recommend. She has experience as an editor in publications such as *Obscura*. Terra has had her poetry and play scripts published in *Project Yes* and *Obscura*. Terra is also currently working towards publishing her collection of short stories, artwork, and poems. A Colorado native, she resides in a small mountain town with her husband and their two sons. You can follow Terra on Instagram *@terraiverson*.

Brice Maiurro (he/him) is the founding editor of South Broadway Press. He is the former Poetry Editor of Suspect Press. He has published two collections of poems, *Stupid Flowers* and *Hero Victim Villain*. You can find him on Instagram *@maiurro*.

Huascar Medina, (he/him) Poet Laureate of Kansas (2019-2021), is the Lit Editor for *seveneightfive* magazine and an Op-Ed writer for *Kansas Reflector*. He's published two collections of poetry *Un Mango Grows in Kansas* (2020) and *How to Hang the Moon* (2017). His words have appeared in *The New York Times, Latino Book Review* and elsewhere.

Sarah Rodriguez is a poet, editor, and Elementary school teacher currently living and teaching in Southwest Denver.

Thank You

A special thank you to Mohaddeseh Seyyed Nouri for the beautiful artwork depicted on the cover of the book.

Also, thank you to LiveWork Denver, whose support was critical to making this project a reality.

Our list of people and organizations to thank for making this book a reality is long and ongoing.

Please visit www.soboghoso.org/dwellthankyou to see everyone involved in this wonderful project.

www.soboghoso.org